Reuben Eneze

I0165032

The Extended Family System in Igbo Culture

The Extended Family System in Igbo Culture

A Social Security System

Reuben Kezie Eneze

Reuben K. Eneze
10402 Meadowridge Lane
Bowie MD, 20721-2854
U.S.A.

© 2019 Reuben Kezie Eneze. All rights reserved.

No part of this book may be reproduced, stored in a retrieval system, or transmitted by any means without the written permission of the author.

ISBN: 978-1-7335505-0-5 (sc)
ISBN: 978-1-7335505-1-2 (e)

Print information available on the last page.

This book is printed on acid-free paper.

Because of the dynamic nature of the Internet, any web addresses or links contained in this book may have changed since publication and may no longer be valid. The views expressed in this work are solely those of the author and do not necessarily reflect the views of the publisher, and the publisher hereby disclaims any responsibility for them.

About the Book

This family system was instituted in Igboland by Igbo ancestors several centuries before European influence on the African West Coast. The system has since survived the evil effects of inter-community wars and slave raids; slave trade, and European colonial activities on the West Coast.

The extended family system established a relatively stable community-life in Igboland through the norms of the traditional marriage institution and the close watch of the elders, who ensured that their ancestral vision was achieved. The system forestalled avoidable marriage break-ups and inter-family squabbles through inbuilt fundamental traditional safeguards. In its early days the system approved of polygamy, when necessary as a means of ensuring family survival or socioeconomic strength. It nurtured centuries-old Igbo ancestral brotherhood and traditional socio-political orientation.

During peace and war times, the system ensured the protection of kin properties such as human life, family names, ancestral land, wives, husbands, children, wealth, statuses, etc. ; and promoted their preservation from one generation to the other. The system also ensured the continuity of the reciprocal assistance and expressive nature of the system . This expression is seen in the visits and physical support given to extended family members during festivals and crises periods.

In recent years there has been modernization on peripheral topics of the system but the major traditional issues of giving and receiving, and the exchange of visits in the Igbo traditional marriage culture has been preserved.

Today, the need for maintaining peaceful interaction in the Igbo family system is always emphasized during cultural meetings.

Dr. Mrs. A.V. Iwueke
Imo State Politechnic
Umuagwo-Ohaji, Imo State, Nigeria

Dedication

To my great-grand twin-daughters,

**Akunna Judith and
Chidi Consolata Ejekwumadu**

Acknowledgement

My gratitude goes to my son-in-law Chinedu and his wife Uche Okeke for their love and kindness to me and my wife Ngozi during these years we have been with them, enjoying the extended family benefits.

I send my special acknowledgment of the love we share to all the members of the Eneze family.

I am deeply grateful to my Missionary friend, Luis Paul S. Baron - SSP, for his generous assistance to me during the proof reading and publication of this book.

Contents

Introduction -   **12**

Chapter 1: Human Family System
1.1 The Earliest Human Family System - - - - -14
1.2 The Earliest Igbo Community - - - - - - - - - 15
1.3 From The Hills To The River-Basins - - - - -17

Chapter 2: Igbo Ethnic Group Of Southern
          Nigeria - - - - - - - - - - - - - - - - - - -19
2.1 Who Are The Igbo? - - - - - - - - - - - - - - -19
2.2 Igbo Settlements - - - - - - - - - - - - - - - - 20
2.3 Are The Igbo of Hebrew (Jewish)Ancestry?22

Chapter 3: Igbo Civilization - - - - - - - - - - - -27
3.1 Ugwuele Culture (Early Stone Age To
     Middle Stone Age) - - - - - - - - - - - - - - - 27
3.2 Scarp-lands Culture (Middle Stone Age To
     Early Iron Age) 2500BC – AD.800 - - - - - - 27
3.3 Nri Culture (A Ritualized Kingship
     Culture) AD800-AD1700 - - - - - - - - - - - -28
3.4 Aro Culture (Slave Trade To Colonization)
     AD1700-1850 - - - - - - - - - - - - - - - - - - -29
3.5 Colonial Culture (Colonization And
     Exploitation) AD 1750-AD 1914 - - - - - - - -30

Chapter 4: Concept Of The Family - - - - - - - - 33
4.1 Family In Igbo Culture - - - - - - - - - - - - - 33
4.2 Male Kinship Matrix - - - - - - - - - - - - - - 36
4.3 Female Kinship Matrix - - - - - - - - - - - - -37

**Chapter 5: Protection Of The Human Family
System (A Comparative Study)** - - -40
5.1 African Effort - - - - - - - - - - - - - - - - - - - 40
5.2 American Effort - - - - - - - - - - - - - - - - - -42

Chapter 6: The Extended Family System - - - -44
6.1 The Establishment Of The Extended
Family System - - - - - - - - - - - - - - - - - - 44

**Chapter 7: Characteristics Of The Extended
Family System** - - - - - - - - - - - - - 46

**Chapter 8: The Marriage Institution As A Basis
For The Extension Of The Human
Family System** - - - - - - - - - - - - - - 49

**Chapter 9: Contracting A Traditional Marriage
In Igbo Culture** - - - - - - - - - - - - - 51
9.1 Finding A Wife (Nchọta Nwanyi) - - - - - - -51
9.2 Suitor's First Contact (Ajụjụ Nwanyi) - - - -52
9.3 Suitors 2nd Visit (Ibu Nmanya Ụmụnne) - 54
9.4 Bride-Wealth In Igbo Culture
(Enwe wanyi) -55
9.5 Suitor's 3nd Visit (Ime Enwe Nwanyi) - - - 57

9.6 Suitor's 4th Visit (Ibu Nmanya Umunna) -59

9.7 Bride's First Official Visit To Suitor
(Ineta Uno) -60
9.8 Suitor's Visit To Bride's Maternal
Grandparents (Ọmụ lụ Beonye)? - - - - - - -61

9.9 Final Marriage Rite (Igbankwụ Nwanyi) - 62

**Chapter 10: Child Adoption In The Igbo
Family System - - - - - - - - - - - - - 66**

**Chapter 11: Evaluation Of The Extended
Family System As Established
By Our Ancestors - - - - - - - - - - - - 71**

**Chapter 12: Erosion Of The Extended
Family System - - - - - - - - - - - - - 74**

References - 82

Introduction

Born in 1937 at Ihe Shikeaguma town, one of the core Igbo culture communities in Southeastern Nigeria, I lived in this community for more than sixty years before I traveled to the USA where this book is written. I personally witnessed and have been in the working of the extended family system in Igbo culture during this period. As a great- grandfather, I have a cultural duty to pass on this experience of the working of the extended family system in Igbo culture to Igbo youths and my readers in this brief write-up.

In this topic, "the extended family system in Igbo culture," I shall initially introduce the Igbo ethnic group of Southern Nigeria to readers. A brief commentary shall be made on who the people of the Igbo ethnic group are, their settlement and their civilization, up to the integration of the Igbo ethnic group into the Nigerian nation by the British colonial office in 1914. Having introduced the Igbo nation to my readers, a brief commentary on the concept of the family to the Igbo shall be made with reference to the male and female kinship matrices which are the corner stones of the extended family system. Then I shall go on to the establishment of the extended family system by Igbo ancestors many centuries ago, with emphasis on what they aimed at achieving by the establishment of this system. Also readers shall be taken to a comparative study of human effort in the protection of the human family system, with emphasis on African and American efforts.

The marriage institution as the basis for the extension of the human family system shall be fully discussed in detail. I shall emphasize on the various stages of the long negotiating time of contracting a traditional marriage in Igbo culture; which was intentionally stretched out by the ancestors to forestall hasty decisions and unnecessary marriage breakups that could lead to inter-family disputes. In order to protect all members of the family system, the ancestors established the adoption of homeless or orphaned children as a further effort towards the strengthening of the extended family system. This adoption of babies by the marriage institution was meant to ensure that homeless children are given parental love and care while childless parents are consoled with the adoption of unwanted babies or children of poor parents.

In concluding the book, the various issues that expose the extended family system to erosion by foreign cultures and values shall be discussed. What should be done to avert this situation shall also be proffered.

Chapter One

HUMAN FAMILY SYSTEM

1.1 The Earliest Human Family System

The human family system started after our earliest ancestors were created. Originally they lived as gatherers of forest roots and vegetables. Later in their wondering life they became subsistence farmers and hunters. They settled in small family units within small settlements far apart from one another. As they migrated from one place to the other in search of food and safety, their population increased. In time, villages, towns and clans emerged. In most cases, family connections were maintained within each settlement. Traditional rules of living were established by each settlement according to its cultural needs. They recognized and respected family origins and gave mutual protection and assistance to each other for the purpose of building a strong and sociable society.

Communities honored their ancestors and worshiped their deities in line with their beliefs. They established traditional festivals and built cultural centers according to their environmental needs and inspiration. They conducted traditional marriage ceremonies in line with their culture. Close and distant family members, where possible, were usually consulted, and invited during marriage ceremonies. The longer a settlement lasted in one location, the deeper and wider the roots of its extended family system went. This system kept family connections alive and provided a traditional platform for its sociopolitical administration led by community elders and titled leaders.

Apart from attacks from wild animals and raids from hostile neighbors over the ownership or the boundaries of land, the ancestors lived in relative peace and traded by barter peacefully on farm and forest produce. Their extended family system was always kept alive as a mobilization tool during peace and war times.

1.2 The Earliest Igbo Community.

The earliest Igbo community lived as one large extended family made up of several clans (Mba). Each clan was composed of several towns (Obodo), while each town was made up of villages (Ama). Each village contained several mega families (umunna). A mega family in turn was made up of several nuclear families of husband, wife and children.

This community was strongly tied together by one language of several mutually intelligible dialects, one traditional religion having various deities, and one political system which had its mobilization strength in the effectiveness of the community's composite parts.

The earliest Igbo community did not have one central political authority or king. Each social unit had its own political leadership that was free of external control but was tied to the Igbo republican system. As long as citizens and neighbors respected the Igbo traditional laws, this political system guaranteed relative peace which protected the freedom of speech, freedom of movement, freedom of worship and freedom of economic pursuit to all. It did not preach or practice political expansion by the use of force. However there were inter-family squabbles and inter village border skirmishes over the ownership or boundaries of land, that were usually settled by the elders.

The boundaries of ancestral community-land were usually clearly demarcated with large trees, huge stones, gullies, brooks, rivers, hills or other natural landmarks. These boundary marks were usually recognized by the elders who were respected as community judges and the ambassadors of the ancestors. These boundary marks were important to the community because the earliest Igbo community lived in village units that were often of same ancestral connection. These settlements developed with time into towns and clans maintaining their original ancestral names and sharing large parcels of ancestral community-land. Each political unit had the right of ownership over the parcel of land on which it lived but also had the duty to protect the original boundaries of that ancestral land.

1.3 From The Hills To The River-Basins

The earliest Igbo were subsistence farmers and part-time hunters. Each village had its own parcel of the ancestral community-land which was usually shared by the mega families and finally into individual parcels of private land. These private parcels of land were of great economic value because each one could be sold for money, exchanged for some other property, mortgaged as a collateral in a debt situation or given as part of the bride-wealth for a wife.

As the families of villages grew in size and number, land occupied by each community became insufficient for farming and habitation. Capable members of affected families moved to new settlements in search of farmland and new occupations. This situation resulted in the movement of members of the Igbo ethnic group in small trickles into the alluvial lands of the Cross, Imo, Anambra and the lower Niger river basins. This movement also exposed the Igbo to other immigrant ethnic peoples from other West African nationalities and enhanced the production of palm produce, yams, spices and other economic and food crops by Igbo farmers, who sold these farm and forest produce to the earliest European traders on the African West Coast.

From the exportation of palm produce and other food crops to the European traders the Igbo joined the lucrative business of the African West Coast which lured the Igbo into the slave trade. Unfortunately the Igbo who reluctantly joined the slave trade later lost thousands of their able bodied sons and daughters each year to the evil trade for two centuries. Today the slave trade has inflicted an unforgettable pain and indelible stripes on the culture and philosophy of the Igbo nation.

Chapter Two

IGBO ETHNIC GROUP OF SOUTHERN NIGERIA

2.1 Who Are The Igbo?

The Igbo are the Igbo-speaking ethnic group of Southern Nigeria and one of the earliest and largest ethnic groups in Africa. The exact ancestral origin of the Igbo ethnic group is not yet well known but through the research work of Archaeologists and Anthropologists, it is established that the earliest ancestors of the Igbo ethnic group settled at Ugwuele in Okigwe Division of Abia State of Southeastern Nigeria as far back as 200,000 BC (Onwuejeogwu 1987).

The Sangonans were forest dwellers occupying the great lakes of Central Africa, the present day Congo and Angola, and around the Zambezi river. They probably spread into different areas in the forest zones of West Africa. This resulted in the development of variants of stone cultures found in West Africa of different ages as shown by the Archaeological findings in Ugwuele,

> *55,000 BC (Anozie 1980) Nsukka*
> *2,555 BC (Hartle 1967 and 1972) Iwo*
> *Eleru 7,250 BC (Shaw 1965[1]).*

From the Ugwuele Stone-age Settlement, the Igbo community has developed into one of Africa's most economically, politically and physically vibrant nations. Today the Igbo can be found in all the cities of the world doing business.

2.2 Igbo Settlements

For millions of years beginning from the early Stone Age to the early Iron Age civilizations, the Igbo had consistently settled in thatched mud-houses at Ugwuele and its environs; in the highland areas of what has come to be known as greater Okigwe, Awgu, Udi, Nsukka and Awka divisions of Southeastern Nigeria.

> *One finds in this region a continuity of cultural development illustrated by the fact that the Afikpo pottery of about 3'000 BC resembles the pottery of present-day Afikpo, while the 'ichi' face marks found on terra cotta heads of nineth century AD Igboukwu resemble the 'ichi' face marks of present- day Umunri[2].*

---

1 M A Onwuejeogwu, Ahiajoku Lecture 1987, Page 15
2 D C Ohadike 1994, Page 10

The growing population of the Igbo culture area which needed food for existence and land for habitation, moved as farmers, hunters, and tradesmen from the highlands to the fertile low lands of the Cross, Anambra, Imo and the lower Niger river basins. During this period of habitation, the Igbo community was joined by various immigrant groups, who came into the Igbo settlements in small trickles, from other stone cultures scattered in West and Central Africa at that time.

As the Saharan region was drying up due to long periods of drought (5000 BC-2500 BC) and its inhabitants needed more fertile and wetter vegetation for farming, there were population movements into the wetter parts of West Africa in general and the already growing Igbo settlements in particular. They came as farm-settlers, laborers, craftsmen, herdsmen, fishermen, hunters, diviners or refugees running away from famine, epidemics, inter-settlement wars and other environmental problems. Their offspring settled and naturalized as members of the Igbo community. At this time also, there were movements of people from the Igbo settlements to other West African settlements for one reason or the other.

A major immigrant movement into the Igbo settlement was that of Eri, the ancestor of Nri, who was believed to have a Hebrew background. He sailed down the Anambra river about AD 800, settled at

Agulueri and established a ritualized kingship culture that reigned in Igboland for nine centuries AD 800 - AD - 1700. This culture overhauled the Igbo political philosophy and established a revitalized democratic republican system that granted relative peace, freedom of economic pursuit, equality to Igbo citizens, thereby stabilizing Igbo economy and inter settlement trade relations.

The Igbo were among the earliest West Africans to establish trading relations with Arab and Egyptian traders. These foreign traders in their earliest relations with the Igbo spelled the Igbo name wrongly in their records as Ibo, Iboe, Ebo, Eboe or Heebo. Some of these wrongly spelled names are still used today by some of these foreigners to identify the Igbo ethnic group of Southern Nigeria.

2.3 Are The Igbo Of Hebrew (Jewish) Ancestry?

This question arises from the fact that there are similarities between the Igbo and the Hebrew cultures, especially in their traditional religious beliefs, their enterprising spirit and easy adaptation to new environments. The question can be approached by looking at the earliest evolutionary trends of the Igbo and the Hebrew.

The history of the origin and settlement of the Igbo can be better understood when we look at these issues alongside the origin and settlements of other African

Reuben Eneze

peoples through the eyes of experts on the subject as stated in chapter 2, sections one and two above.

On the other hand, the ancestor and patriarch of the Hebrew, Abraham was born at Ur (Iraq) in Babylon about 2100 BC. His descendants moved to Canaan about 1400 BC and established a Hebrew nation called Israel. Before Abraham was born in Ur Babylon in 2100 BC, the Igbo were settled at Ugwuele in Okigwe Division for several centuries with other West African peoples but had little contact with other parts of Africa.

Eri the ancestor of Nri clan who is believed by the Igbo to have Hebrew background, sailed down the Anambra river about AD 800 and settled at Agulueri. Nri mythology has it that on arrival Eri met Igbo settlers who had no memory of their origin, and noted that the people had no food and no king (Onwuejeogwu 1987).

> Chukwu the Creator
> Sent Eri down.
> Eri came down from the Sky.
> He sailed down the river Anambra,
> And established at Aguleri.
> Mystical powers, he had,
> Which won the people over to him.
> They had no king and
> There was no food.
> Chukwu fed them on firmament etc[3]

Eri probably moved southwards from a Hebrew settlement in North Africa as a diviner during one of the famines that resulted from the drying up of the Saharan region, due to long droughts. His descendants and agents perfected the art of divination. They had great mystical powers and great wealth that won the admiration and respect of the Igbo settlers of the Anambra river basin. They ruled the Igbo for nine centuries AD 800 - 1700, bringing together twelve Igbo settlements under one kingship unit. During this period the Nri overhauled the Igbo culture and established new deities and new taboos in all the areas of their business. They manipulated these ritualized establishments for political and business purposes.

Nri influence in Igboland was much felt in the near East and West of the lower Niger, covering what is now known as Anambra and Delta states of Nigeria. On the hilly and more Eastern parts of the lower Niger basin, covering the present-day Enugu, Ebonyi, Abia, and Imo states of Nigeria, Nri influence was mild because Ugwuele in Uturu Okigwe which is situated in this area was the earliest settlement of Igbo ancestors and the birthplace of Igbo culture. Although archaeological and linguistic evidences of the Ugwuele culture can still be found today within Ugwuele and its environs; there are also evidences of the nine centuries of Nri influence in this area, such as

---

3   M.A. Onwuejeogwu 1987 Ahiajoku Lecture, Page 1

the shrines of Nri deities and oracles. Cultural and political institutions such as traditional title taking were also established by Nri agents in all the settlements under their influence before the arrival of the British to the West Coast of Africa.

When we remember the amount of negligence given to the study and development of Igbo culture for two centuries by the British administration, especially to Igbo language, Igbo traditional religion, Igbo traditional democratic system and Igbo moral value system; as compared to the amount of promotion given to the study of English language and culture by the same administration, for the same period in Nigeria, we will no longer find it difficult to know why Igbo culture is similar to Hebrew culture after nine centuries of Hebrew political and cultural influence in Igboland.

Some scholars argue that the similarity of Igbo names with Hebrew names is proof that the Igbo have same ancestry with the Hebrew. This position is not convincing enough without reference to archaeological, anthropological and linguistic evidences of the Igbo activities in Igboland for several centuries before the birth of Abraham - the ancestor and patriarch of the Hebrew.

My name is Reuben. I am an Igbo man. The similarity of my name with the name of the first son of Jacob (a Hebrew) does not make me a Hebrew.

Let us take another example. When the first Europeans came to America, the native Americans were living in America. The Europeans mistakenly called them Indians. Later they changed the name of their land to America. They colonized the place and brought Africans and other nationalities into America. Within about five centuries they overhauled the culture of the native Americans. Today English and Spanish are among the leading languages spoken in America and European culture is established here, with an admixture of various other cultures including the native American culture. This situation does not make the native Americans Europeans.

Chapter Three

IGBO CIVILIZATION
(BRIEF COMMENTARY)

3.1 Ugwuele Culture (Early Stone Age to Middle Stone Age)

The Ugwuele culture (200,000 BC - 2,500 BC) contained the proto-Igboid period (100,000-5,000 BC) or what I might call, the formative period of Igbo ethnicity and craftsmanship. It was the period of the development of subsistence farming as against the period of gathering forest roots, fruits and vegetables. It was also known for its pottery industry which has existed till today in the Okigwe, Uturu, Inyi, Ugbo, Ozala, and Nsukka areas of Southeastern Nigeria.

3.2 Scarplands Culture (Middle Stone Age To Early Iron Age) 2500 BC - AD 800

The Scarp-lands culture which is also called the Okigwe, Afikpo, Udi and Nsukka era, was an offshoot of the Ugwuele culture. It flourished from the Middle Stone Age through late Stone Age to early Iron Age, evolving into the Iron Age industry that existed within the Nsukka-Udi axis.

This civilization had a rich agrarian and commercial economy based on iron implements, colorful masks, elephant tusks, ivory bracelets and horses from Northern Nigeria.

It developed a traditional democratic political institution which was overhauled and ritualized by the Nri era.

3.3 Nri Culture (A Ritualized Kingship Culture) AD800 – AD1700

Nri culture which was a ritualized kingship culture was often referred to as the civilization of the sacred and the divine by historians because it was believed by the Igbo that the Nri king (Eze Nri derived his legitimacy from God. Nri politics and economic system were ritualized. The concept of peace, truth and harmony was seen in the execution of all its traditional institutions that were also ritualized.

This civilization was one of the greatest and most stabilizing events in the history of the Igbo nation. Some writers of Igbo history suggest that Eri's (ancestor of Nri) ancestors might have had some contacts with some black Jews who migrated southwards into West Africa from North Africa during the drying up of the Saharan lands due to dry conditions, hence the Nri had a sacred kingship system; practiced slavery, human sacrifice and a new version of God worship.

The Nri influence on the Igbo nation, and the arrival of Iduu culture to Western Igboland from Benin led to the establishment of kingship systems in places like Arochukwu, Agbor and Onitsha before the arrival of European influence to Igboland.

3.4 Aro Culture (Slave Trade To Colonization) AD1700-1850

The Aro era was an offshoot of the Nri civilization and contemporaneous with other less popular Iron Age Igbo cultures. Arochukwu, a trading town was founded by Igbo traders from the Southeastern Igbo area who initially traded on palm produce, elephant tusks and spices with European traders. The white traders who came to the West Coast of Africa with a gun in one hand and trading goods on the other hand lured the Aro traders into the slave trade.

Before the onset of slave trade the Aro traders were becoming morally decadent and rich as a result of the new economic position along the West African coast. This civilization through its own moral weakness opened up slave markets in Igboland and supervised the sale of thousands of able-bodied Igbo men and women into slavery. Its cooperation with European slave traders depleted the Igbo wealth of able bodied men and women and weakened the Igbo leadership position in the emerging economic and political prosperity of the lower Niger area.

The Islamic reform movement launched from Sokoto by Arab Muslim leaders in AD 1804 spread to almost every part of Northern Nigeria generating wars that produced thousands of captives for the slave market. The Aro slave traders acted as middlemen between the Arab slave traders from Northern Nigeria and the European traders on the West African coast. Other ethnic groups in West Africa took part in the slave trade but the Aro slave traders monopolized one of the major slave trade routes in West Africa by the middle of the 18th century.

The Aro civilization lasted only one and a half centuries (AD 1700-1850) yet it left ugly and indelible marks on the culture and philosophy of the Igbo nation.

3.5 Colonial Culture (Colonization And Exploitation) AD1750 – AD1914

By the middle of the 18th century the Igbo nation had emerged as a distinct people with one language and was occupying a geographical area covering parts of the lower Niger, Anambra, Imo and Cross river basins. She had both political and economic influence in the area now known as southeastern and south southern Nigeria. By this time the Igbo nation was playing a leading role in the emerging European trade within the fast growing export trade of the African West Coast. Large quantities of arms and ammunition were exchanged for export goods of the African West Coast.

By AD 1850 tens of thousands of able bodied men and women were killed in inter-settlement wars and European instigated and financed slave raids, or carried away into slavery. The Igbo nation which had no central government and no standing army had enjoyed relative peace and economic stability for about nine centuries during the Nri civilization, and could not face the military onslaught of the British imperial might. Each Igbo community was left to defend itself according to its defense capability using its traditional defense tactics such as gorilla war tactics.

After the reduction of Igbo wealth of able-bodied men and women through slave trade the British who had enjoyed the wealth of the African West Coast through trade now decided to colonize and exploit the wealth of the African West Coast. The British got treaties of protection negotiated and signed with some Igbo community leaders and took to swift military expeditions to silence the small remaining units of Igbo resistance.

Between AD 1700 and 1900 the devastating effect of the slave trade on Igbo culture and civilization was total and final. The ancestors of the Igbo were beaten hands-down by European canons and guns between AD 1880 and 1920, the longest history of European resistance in Africa south of the Sahara apart from that of the Zulu (Onwuejeogwu 1987)[4].

It took the British over twenty years of constant military action to subdue the Igbo who flung themselves against the British with only cap guns, dane guns and machetes. The Igbo were slaughtered in their thousands by the British rifles and machine guns with unlimited supplies of ammunition (Elizabeth Isichei)[5].

By 1914, the Nigerian nation was created by the British colonial office and the Igbo nation was integrated into this new nation as part of Eastern Nigeria. Today it is made up of five states of Abia, Anambra, Ebonyi, Enugu and Imo; including pockets of ethnic Igbo towns in parts of the surrounding communities of Delta, Rivers, Cross River and Kogi states of Nigeria.

---

4   M. A. Onwuejeogwu, 1987 Ahiajoku Lecture, Page 1
5   Elizabeth Isichei, A history of the Igbo people.

Chapter Four

CONCEPT OF THE FAMILY

4.1 Family In Igbo Culture

The family in Igbo culture is a fundamental social unit made up of a man and a woman united in marriage for the procreation of children and for the extension of the human family system. In Igbo culture, a formal traditional marriage is the basis for starting a new family unit. The meticulous precautions taken and the traditional rites observed during the institution of this union underlines the importance of the family system to Igbo culture and philosophy. All these precautions are aimed at protecting the Igbo family system and the marriage institution so that every Igbo child is born in a secure home where he/she is welcome and brought up by the parents in his/her family as a legitimate and acceptable member of the family and the community. These children of the Igbo nuclear families grow up and start new families of their own that become the extended family units of the Igbo community.

In Igbo culture parents (man and woman) are ambassadors of the ancestors in their family units and are traditionally duty bound to guide their children on the right path in the worship of God and the respect of traditional laws. On their part children are bound to love, respect and obey their parents and all elders in the community. The Igbo community with respect to its family norms ensures that everybody works hard and provides support for the individual, the family and by extension the Igbo community. In Igbo tradition, the family is a sacred institution ordained by God for the procreation and protection of the human race. In Igboland during the precolonial days, the family homestead was seen as a sacred abode of the ancestors and deities especially in those areas of Igboland where the ancestors were buried in their homes that also contained shrines and altars of their deities.

Several traditional laws were made by the Igbo ancestors to protect the Igbo homestead from any violation of the traditional family norms by residents and strangers alike because each family was seen in Igbo culture as a foundation block of the Igbo community. Culturally, the family constitutes the first training ground for the community's human resources and the first level of the Igbo traditional government. It is the first traditional rallying point and a mobilization unit for spiritual and sociopolitical purposes in the Igbo community.

The Igbo traditional love of the family is expressed in the fact that every Igboman proudly bears his father's or paternal grandfather's name as his family name and will take all the pains there is to protect the family name from any abuse. He has great attachment to his father's ancestral home and will consider its welfare a top priority in the list of his spiritual, educational, infrastructural and sociopolitical projects. On the other hand every Igbo person sees his/her mother's ancestral family as an important resort and as an inseparable part of his/her mother that must be loved and respected. The essence of this traditional structuring of the Igbo family system by the ancestors was to provide a social system where every body is his/her brother's/sister's keeper.

In this system, no homeless baby was welcome, because it was a liability to the mother, the family and by extension the Igbo nation. Such a baby's safety and adequate upbringing was not always assured because it was an abomination in Igbo culture for a woman to bear a baby outside of marriage. The Igbo traditional moral value-system saw such a woman as a wayward person and her baby as an illegitimate baby. The illegitimate status was placed on the baby by traditional law as a punishment to the mother and her family, to drive home the Igbo traditional condemnation of promiscuous sex-life and the violation of the Igbo traditional family norms.

In many parts of Igboland all family land belonged to the male members of the kinship units. Male children of unmarried mothers in these areas did not have the right of inheritance on any such land or economic trees in their mothers' ancestral homes. In their fathers' homes (if known), such children were not welcome and were treated as strangers until bride wealth was paid and other traditional marriage rites were performed on their mothers by the men responsible for fathering the children.

The Igbo love large family units that sometimes include adopted children and members of other extended family units. These large units could be made up of grand children, grandparents, parents-in-law, cousins, widows and orphaned relatives who live under one male family head, where they are sheltered from the effect of poverty, oldage or illness. The male children of each family unit are taught to act together in their day-to-day activities and to love one another as members of one kinship unit (Umunna).

4.2 Male Kinship Matrix

The male kinship matrix (Umunna) is made up of the males in a single ancestral family unit. They share one ancestor from which their nuclear families originate and develop into other extended family units. These units oftentimes grow into villages, towns and clans. In precolonial days most members of a male kinship matrix lived on their ancestral land in their neighborhood. They got married to women from other units and started new families as members of the extended families of their own ancestor. They shared their ancestral name, social facilities and mutual assistance. The male children of a man called "Agu", for example, got married, had many children and his family grew into a mega family called ("Umuagu") Agu's children. This mega family developed into a village called 'Amagu' (Agu's village) before splitting up into new 'Amagu' sub villages that later grew into towns.

The sub villages of Agu's ancestral family unit could bear names like Amagu Highland (Amagu Ugwu), Amagu Lowland (Amagu Agbo) and Amagu Central (Amagu Etiti). These new villages will grow into new towns that will make up the Amagu clan which will bear a name like (Amaguato or Mbaato). Three village town.

In precolonial days new village settlements having one ancestral name were built up communally with little extra cost on the individual owners of the new homes. Community facilities such as roads, markets, worship centers, waterfronts, civic centers and play grounds were also built and maintained communally with due reference to, and approval of ancestral elders. Economic activities like farming, fishing, hunting etc, were handled in groups by village units or trade guilds, yet each family unit maintained the ownership of its parcels of land, the proceeds from its land and the share of games from fishing and hunting.

4.3 Female Kinship Matrix

The female kinship matrix (Umuada) in Igbo culture is made up of all the female offspring of a family or ancestral unit. These females grow up and get married within or outside their ancestral units. They take up their husband's family names and help to set up their own nuclear families that develop within their husband's kinship connections far away from the family of their birth.

This traditional movement of members of the female kinship matrix from the family units of their birth for marriage to other ancestral units is the main reason for Igbo preference of male to female children; to ensure that there is a care-taker for the paternal ancestral home and the continuation of its extended family system. However this movement of the female offspring to marriage in different directions create scattered clusters of female blood-relatives that help to make up the female kinship matrix. These clusters may be geographically separated by marriage but they are closely tied to the extended family system of their paternal ancestral units by blood affinity. They constitute the powerful female kinship units (Umuada) in Igbo culture that share great mutual respect with their male counterparts in their paternal ancestral units.

The children of the female offspring share mutual respect, moral sanctions, protection and socio-economic assistance with members of their mothers' ancestral units in addition to their rights, obligations and duties in their own fathers' families and ancestral kinship connections. The husbands of members of the female kinship matrix in addition to their own ancestral duties and responsibilities at home owe a debt of bride price and other sociocultural duties to their in-laws. In Igbo culture the bride wealth on a wife is never complete until her death. The bride wealth could be demanded at any time from the husband in the form of mutual respect and assistance. The female kinship matrix continues to grow until the fifth generation (in some Igbo communities) when members of the male and female kinship matrices can intermarry in the same ancestral unit without the fear of the sin of incest.

Chapter Five

PROTECTION OF THE HUMAN FAMILY SYSTEM (A COMPARATIVE STUDY)

5.1 African Effort

During the slave trade the family system in Africa went through great social disruptions and abuses. The extended family system which had taken root in many parts of Africa was threatened with total destruction. There were slave raids and inter-settlement wars instigated by local hirelings and facilitated with arms and ammunition by the slave masters from Europe who bought the war captives as slaves.

Family farms were deserted and crop failures became widespread. Local markets were closed down or reduced in size and number. The usual boisterous African village-life became quiet and somber. Many children were abandoned by, killed or abducted parents. Tired and sick elders who were earlier respected and honored as representatives of the ancestors were abandoned by fleeing or abducted relatives. Many families were afflicted with famine, poverty, illness, death and bereavement. Entire villages were threatened with extermination by the brutal human trade and inter-settlement wars that ravaged many parts of Africa at that time.

Surviving members of rural communities were forced by this situation to protect their families from extermination due to constant slave raids. Groups of families moved close together in more compact village units and armed themselves with available locally produced arms against the invaders. Compound walls or fences were made, or reinforced by each family to stop or slow down attackers and wild animals from forced entries into their family compounds. Family and ancestral connections were more closely watched and protected. Kinship connections were reinforced to include surviving members of the extended family no matter how far apart. Each person became his/her brother's/sister's keeper. Some of these earliest survival measures were constantly reviewed and strengthened in line with the needs of each settlement.

Eventually some of these measures have remained the traditional laws of the extended family system in many parts of Africa today. Although the creation of the extended family system was a slow process and took centuries to mature, it has survived great tremors from tribal wars, slave trade and European colonial activities in Africa.

In many parts of Africa today evidence of the protection measures taken by our ancestors to protect the family from forced entries during slave raids and tribal wars can still be seen in the continued construction of compound walls and fences everywhere even in the urban centers. This desire to continue to wall-in residential compounds makes it look like the fear of forced entries which was the order of the day during the slave-raid-years has refused to depart the memories of men.

5.2 American Effort

The desire to protect the family has always moved humanity to protective action not only in Africa but also in other parts of the world at all times. In the United States of America for instance, the same desire to protect its retired workers and their families from financial insecurity necessitated the creation and maintenance of the Social Security system.

As early as the middle of the 19th century, fast-industrial growth started in America. Farmers who were self sufficient in food production in the rural areas migrated to industrial centers in search of work in the industries away from family and friends. In addition to these workers was a large number of immigrant industry-workers from other parts of the world who usually left friends and families thousands of miles behind. Most of them came to America with nothing other than the clothes on their bodies and the suit cases or haversacks in their hands. Millions of these industry workers were entirely dependent on their meager wages. They worked for long hours daily with little pay and no job security. This situation resulted in many workers' strikes for more pay. There was instability in industry in America at that time.

Faced with the economic crises created by workers unrest and the possibility of a massive social upheaval created by this situation and the Great Depression, President Franklin Roosevelt and congress created a system of retirement benefits called Social Security in 1935.
Initially the system was intended to

> □*Provide financial security for older American workers usually expended and forgotten by their employers*

> □ *Help compensate for limited job opportunities available to older people in the society*

> □ *Bridge the financial gap created by the need for American workers to move around the country in search of decent employment.*

> □ *Help provide financial assistance to displaced workers and their families*

The social security as created by Roosevelt in 1935 has since been constantly reviewed and strengthened with interrelated measures to cover all American workers and their families.

Chapter Six

THE EXTENDED FAMILY SYSTEM

6.1 The Establishment Of The Extended Family System.

The extended family system in Igbo culture is a social security institution that was established many centuries before the birth of Jesus Christ by Igbo ancestors. It was established to administer a number of interrelated social issues such as marriage and family relations for the economic and physical protection of the Igbo family system.

The elders who established the system, charged it with the social obligation to establish cultural measures that would among other things:

a) Supervise and protect the marriage institution through inbuilt fundamental traditional safeguards to avoid marriage breakups and the consequent exposure of children to parental abuses.

b) Provide through the marriage institution a legitimate and socially secure home for every child in his/her father's home where adequate parental upbringing would be assured.

c) Ensure that through the marriage institution there was an alternative but temporal home in the maternal ancestral family for every person in case of a serious social misunderstanding, dispute or social disturbance in his/her paternal family.

d) Provide humanitarian assistance through family connections to all members of the extended family faced with the problems of bereavement, orphanhood, poverty, disability, illness, old age or retirement.

e) Provide physical protection and economic assistance to all through community service.

f) Encourage members of the Igbo family system to give help and protection to all other members of their extended family outside home or in foreign lands.

g) Forestall the erosion of the extended family system by foreign cultures and values.

Chapter Seven

CHARACTERISTICS OF THE EXTENDED FAMILY SYSTEM

The extended family system in its structural nature has clusters of immediate and remote relatives. Among the immediate relatives are father, mother and unmarried children who live in one household or adjacent to it. This residence sometimes also houses distant blood relatives such as orphaned cousins, elderly in-laws, and house-hands who live under one elder in an extended family unit. Members include other kins of a lineal nature and relatives of collateral character who owe allegiance to a common ancestor. This type of relationship includes people who descend from distant ancestors, and those who descend from two separate ancestors, as in children of women married to men from distant ancestors and vise-versa.

Every extended family unit has an elder or a titled person who acts as the corporate head, and is also respected as the ambassador of the ancestors. He has command over that ancestral family unit. His house is the center for most extended family issues such as rituals and socio-political activities. This kinship system manifests its expressive and corporate nature in the protection of kin properties such as land, wives, husbands, children, wealth, statuses etc; and ensures their preservation from one generation to the other. A number of nuclear families as composed above live in one settlement in their ancestral land and make up sub village units that eventually develop into large villages, towns and clans. As the villages and towns grow and split into many families so also the extended family connections grow in number and space. The various units so formed bear the names of the ancestors that were once corporate heads or titled leaders of the various units of the extended family system. These ancestors are honored and celebrated in all Igbo communities during annual festivals or family days.

Though marriage and residential distance may intensify the collateral character of some units of the extended family system, this situation does not remove the reciprocal assistance and expressive nature of the system. In Igboland the expressive nature of the extended family system is seen in the visits and the physical support given to members during festivals and crises periods. Members of the Igbo family units at home or abroad try to keep in close touch with the family elders of their ancestral families at home for prayers and advice before taking serious decisions affecting their lives, such as marriages, career changes, important business deals, or political engagements.

Members of the extended family units in Igboland have joint ownership of such things as land, for residence, farming, grazing, hunting, fishing, worship, markets, schools, village squares etc. Most of these parcels of land exist within their ancestral villages or towns and are named after their ancestors as in (Ani Umuagu) land of the children of Agu. Most of these parcels of land were acquired and preserved by the ancestors for centuries, for the use of their children. All the children who inherit these parcels of land also inherit the common responsibility to continue to preserve these ancestral parcels of land, to ensure the appropriate use of such parcels of land.

In precolonial times most of the inter town struggles and disputes in those days resulted from the establishment of the ownership or boundaries of parcels of ancestral land. In order to forestall the possibility of border wars or litigations the elders of neighboring communities of the disputing villages or towns usually came together and after hearing from both sides established the ownership or boundaries of land. They used landmarks such as rivers, roads, trees or stones as beacons.

Chapter Eight

THE MARRIAGE INSTITUTION AS A BASIS FOR THE EXTENSION OF THE HUMAN FAMILY SYSTEM

In Igbo culture it is believed that marriage is a sacred partnership between a man and a woman established by God for the extension of the human family system. Neither the man nor the woman alone is a complete unit in this business of extending the human family system. Each of these two people needs the other to implement the work of God's creation of the human person. In the day-to-day activities of the family, God has given man ample energy and disposition to be the family-head and breadwinner while the woman is equipped to bear and nurse the babies, and to assist the man in the running of the family.

The ancestors recognized these facts and took their time to structure the traditional marriage institution with inbuilt precautions and safeguards against marriage breakups and the accompanying problems. These safeguards were attached in order to ensure the continuity and extension of the human family system. To achieve these objectives, contracting a traditional marriage in Igboland was structured to take a long negotiating time in order to involve other members of both families, and to ensure that there has been genuine mutual visits and gifts by both the male and female partners who go into the marriage pact. These acts of giving and receiving indicate to both their families that the male and the female are willing and ready to embark on the joint venture of marriage.

To ensure these marriage norms are respected, two third-party persons (witnesses), one from each of the sides are selected to represent the Igbo community to ensure that the marriage tradition is adhered to especially in the areas of mutual visits and gifts. In the event of a disagreement or a marriage breakup, the two third-party persons and an equal number of elders from both sides to the marriage constitute the traditional marriage council in Igboland, and their decisions are usually respected. These traditional marriage norms still remain strong and binding on both parties to a traditional marriage in Igboland irrespective of the incursion of external influences or modernization. In various communities of Igboland additional measures are taken to ensure that smooth and successful marriages meet up the sacred vision of our ancestors towards the smooth extension of the Igbo family system.

Chapter Nine

CONTRACTING A TRADITIONAL MARRIAGE IN IGBO CULTURE

9.1 Finding A Wife (Nchọta Nwanyi)

In Ihe Shikeaguma and many other communities of Enugu state of Nigeria for instance, a suitor takes the following steps in contracting a traditional marriage.

Finding the right girl that meets the needs of the proposed husband and his family is the first task. In Igbo culture, parents, male and female have an important part to play in the finding or giving approval of prospective wives for their children. During precolonial years when there were no formal schools, parents arranged marriage partners for their children. Betrothed girl-child wives as young as five to ten years old were brought up together with their boy-child husbands by parents-in- law who wanted to help in shaping the character of their prospective daughters-in-law.

This arrangement had its weaknesses because some girls grew up and rejected their betrothed boy-child husbands or their parents and vice-versa. Though many such arrangements succeeded, the betrothal of girl-child wives in Igboland has gone out of fashion because boys and girls now go to school and leave primary and secondary schools as young adults and prefer to select their own future spouses by themselves. Now parents have no other choice but to advise their children and educate them on how to choose their future spouses; and give them moral and financial support. Parents and other members of the extended families often times make suggestions of good marriageable girls to their prospective suitors. When the young suitors make up their minds they come back to their parents for support.

9.2 Suitor's First Contact (Ajụjụ Nwanyi)

If parents or guardians approve of the choice of a particular girl by their son, they make the first contact by sending a third-party person, who could be a member of their extended family or a trusted friend who knows both the families well to make this contact. The third-party person could be a man or a woman who usually goes to indicate the intention of the prospective suitor's parents to visit the prospective bride's parents. If the suitor's parent's proposal is accepted by the girl's parents, the suitor's parents are asked to come, and a date is fixed for this first visit.

On the appointed date, the suitor's parents or guardians arrive with the suitor and the third-party person. They carry with them some kola nuts and about two gallons of palm wine, for the girl's parents. The father of the girl receives the kola nuts and palm wine with thanks, and prays to God and the ancestors for the success of this proposal. The kola nuts and the palm wine are shared with the prospective in-laws who are usually entertained with food. After this entertainment the visitors are asked to discuss their intention. At this stage the parents of the girl do not reject or accept the proposal but they ask for time to interview their daughter.

They usually use this time to interview the girl, make family consultations and investigate family records of the intended suitor and his parents. If the investigations and consultations are positive, the parents of the girl send a message of invitation through the third-party person to the parents of the suitor for a second visit. If no message is received after about one month, the parents of the suitor usually assume that their request is refused. If an invitation is sent to the family of the intended suitor to come and hear the result of the investigation carried out by the father of the bride, the indication is usually an acceptance of the suitor's request.

9.3 Suitors' Second Visit (Ibu Nmanya Umunne)

The parents of the suitor in the company of their son and the third-party person make the second visit carrying an increased number of kola nuts and gallons of palm wine for their nuclear family and the closer members of the extended family. After entertaining the suitor and his family with food and drinks, the father of the girl announces that his investigations were positive. He presents a cup of palm wine to his daughter for her to confirm her acceptance of the suitor's proposal. She usually presents the cup of palm wine after taking a sip of it, to the suitor. If the suitor accepts and drinks the palm wine, both families rejoice over the mutual acceptance of the marriage proposal. They congratulate the suitor and the bride on their performance.

With the giving and taking of the symbolic drink, by the suitor and his bride, the suitor's family is informed that they should pay the bride-wealth.

9.4 Bride-Wealth In Igbo Culture (Enwe Nwanyi)

Our ancestors believed that marriage is a sacred partnership between a man and a woman instituted by God for the extension of the human family system. They also believed that each of these two persons, man and woman should show to the elders enough evidence of full commitment to this sacred pact. While the woman should be prepared to leave her family of birth and go to the man of her choice to start another family, the man should show enough preparedness to share his wealth with the woman of his choice and the children of this union by giving a token of his wealth to the parents of his proposed bride.

Since precolonial days bride-wealth has never been meant to be a one time price of a bride, rather it has been a process of giving and receiving in the form of physical, economic and social assistance between the two families involved in the marriage relationship. This mutual giving and taking continues as long as the marriage relationship subsists. It is the substance that usually lubricates the beautiful relationships in the Igbo traditional marriage and the extended family system.

To ensure that the instituted marriage norms of the Igbo community was maintained, the ancestors insisted that one could only share what one had with his wife, hence the Igbo name for bride-wealth, "Enwe" (what one has.). Consequently many items of physical wealth at that time in many parts of Igboland were approved by the elders for bride-wealth. These items included land, economic trees, livestock, clothing, cowries, ornaments, physical assistance etc. At that time, most marriages were contracted between couples of same ancestral villages or towns and fathers-in-law did not have to carry some of their daughters' bride-wealth for long distances to their homes. Also the use of third party persons (Dianu Nwanyi) as witnesses during the payments or repayments of bride-wealth was also established by the elders. This was done as a necessary measure to place a check on the execution of the Igbo traditional marriage norms and to ensure fair play in the handling of the Igbo traditional marriage issues.

After the arrival of European traders to the West African Coast in the 16th century, the medium of exchange changed from barter to the use of money. Traders and white-color workers preferred the use of money to the use of other items of material wealth for the settlement of bride-wealth. This preference was because of the ease with which money was handled, its mobility and its wonderful purchasing power. Before the elders could take a second look at the use of money for the settlement of bride wealth, the slave trade with its myriads of evil effects on the Igbo community-life disrupted the effectiveness of all Igbo social structures. Secondly the demobilization of soldiers at the end of the second world war in 1945 brought a new twist into the handling of the Igbo traditional marriage issues. Thousands of Nigerians who served in the British contingent brought the war-bonus paid to soldiers into Igboland in crisp currency notes. This arrival of new money and the rise in the wealth of the returnee Igbo youths coupled with the hangover of the slave trade did not only formalize the inclusion of money as part of bride- wealth, it also hiked the level of payments of bride-wealth in Igboland. This situation also changed the name of this settlement from bride-wealth to bride price.

9.5 Suitor's Third Visit (Ime Enwe Nwanyi)

After the symbolic drink during the suitors second visit, the bride price is the next issue. The family of the suitor after a meeting on how to handle the payment of the bride- price, invites their third-party person. They send him to the parents of the bride to fix the date for the payment of the bride-price. On the appointed date, the suitor, his third party person and one representative of the suitor's family carry the bride price, some kola nuts, and palm wine to the house of the bride's father. The bride's father invites his own third party person on this important meeting.

Prayers are said by the bride's father or his representative after which the kola nuts and the palm wine are shared by all present. The suitor's third party person presents the bride-price and hands it to the in-law's third party person who counts the money in the presence of everybody, announces the amount and hands it over to the bride's father or his representative. The bride's father thanks the suitor's family, makes a comment such as asking for an increase of the bride price money, before accepting it.

In Ihe Shikeaguma of Enugu State in Nigeria, bride price is usually not negotiated or rejected but the prospective in-law usually asks for an increase of the bride price, no matter how much is paid. This gesture symbolizes the fact that no amount of money is big enough as a human being's price. Usually the suitor's family thanks the bride's family and adds some more money to what was paid or promises to do so in the near future. The bride's father gives 5% of whatever he accepts to his third party person who shares the money with the suitor's third party person as their commission.

The suitor and his family members, including the two third party persons are entertained by the bride's family before they leave for home. In many parts of Igboland bride price is carried by the family of the spouse to the family of the bride while in other parts the family of the bride goes to the family of the spouse to collect the bride price of their daughter. In either case, other members of the extended family and the third party persons are usually involved to ensure compliance with the Igbo traditional marriage norms.

These norms vary a little bit from community to community.

9.6 Suitor's Fourth Visit (Ibu Nmanya Umunna)

The influence of members of the extended family system in all Igbo traditional marriages is further exhibited in the fourth visit of the suitor to the family of the bride. During this visit the suitor's family presents kola nuts and palm wine to the bride's mega family (Umunna) and closer members of the bride's extended family, to inform them of the marriage proposal and to seek their approval and support for same.

In preparation for the visit, the spouse usually sends his third party person to the family of the bride to fix the date for this visit and to ascertain the quantity of the kola nuts and palm wine required for this visit. He also finds out from his family the number of people making the visit with him and uses the number to fix the type and cost of food entertainment that goes with the drinks. He sends the money to the bride's parents through his third party person some days ahead of the visit while he buys the kola nuts and the palm wine. In recent times assorted types of drinks are now included in what is required for the visits of prospective spouses.

On the appointed date, the spouse, his third party person, some members of his mega family and friends carry the required quantity of kola nuts, palm wine and other assorted drinks to the family of the bride.

The kola nuts and drinks are presented to the bride's mega family by an elder from the spouse's family. The bride's family elders inspect and taste the palm wine to ensure that the right type and quantity of drinks have been presented by the spouse. If the bride's elders accept the kola nuts and drinks, they ask the bride's father if he has settled the bride price issue with the spouse. If his answer is yes, prayers are said and entertainment starts with the sharing of the drinks between the two families. After this ceremony the bride can now visit the spouse's family and stay for one or two days to have an idea of what her future home looks like.

In recent times, many suitors live in towns far away from Igboland. To reduce the cost of distant visits by the suitor, they arrange with the bride's family to hold the second and third visits' rites together in one day. Under this arrangement the kola nuts and the palm wine for the two occasions are presented together or partly paid for by the suitor in money terms.

9.7 Bride's First Official Visit To Suitor (Ineta Uno)

Since the bride price on the bride has been paid and the members of her mega family (Ụmụ nna) have been informed of the marriage proposal with the presentation of their kola nuts and palm wine by the spouse's family, the bride is now qualified to officially visit the family of the spouse to see what her future home looks like.

Up to this stage and after this visit the bride and spouse still have the right to change their minds in the marriage proposal. For this reason, the spouse and members of his family do all they can to please the bride. The spouse buys new clothes, shoes and ornaments for the bride and introduces his new bride to his friends. She is showered with praises and presents in cash and kind by friends and members of the extended family of the spouse.

On her own part the bride tries to be nice to everybody introduced to her by the prospective spouse and tries to show her future family members that she really appreciates their kindness and would like to live with them. After one or two days, the bride returns home to her parents.

9.8 Suitor's Visit To Bride's Maternal Grand Parents (Ọmụlụ Be Onye?)

The spouse visits the bride's maternal grandparents to inform them of his marriage proposal with their granddaughter. Although the kola nuts and palm wine for this visit are not much, the visit is important because it helps the spouse to know the ancestral roots of his bride and helps the bride's grandparents to have a glimpse of their grandson-in-law before the final rites of marriage are completed between him and their granddaughter.

The Igbo ancestors who initiated the Igbo traditional marriage act included all these mutual premarital visits to ensure that marriages avoid all stumbling blocks on the way to smooth marital relations and peaceful extended family life.

On this visit, the suitor is accompanied by one or two members of his family and they carry as much kola nuts and palm wine as prescribed by his elders. Usually the bride's grandparents are informed in advance of this visit.

9.9 Final Marriage Rite (Igbankwụ Nwanyi)

The successful completion of contracting the long negotiated Igbo traditional marriage is celebrated during this final marriage rite of presenting kola nuts, and palm wine to the bride's village and the members of her extended family. Before embarking on this visit, the following marriage rites must have been completed:

a) Prayers and consultations have been completed after the first visit, by both the families of the bride and the suitor, and positive results are received from these consultations

b) The suitor and the bride have agreed to marry by the giving and taking of palm wine in the presence of both their families.

c) Both parents of the suitor and the bride have given their blessings to the marriage.

d) Members of both families have been informed by the suitor through the presentation of kola nuts and palm wine.

e) The bride price has been paid to the bride's family and the two witnesses have taken their commission of 5% of the bride price.

f) The bride has officially visited and approved of the suitor's home and people.

g) The suitor has visited the maternal grandparents of the bride and received their blessing of the proposed marriage.

This day of goodbye rite in Igbo traditional marriage is a day of eating and drinking. It is also a day of drumming and dancing for both families of the bride and the suitor with their friends. This is the long awaited day in the lives of every Igbo bride and bridegroom. They put on their best clothes and ornaments with the most fashionable hairstyle affordable. About a month before this ceremony the family of the suitor through their third party persons (witnesses) agrees with the family of the bride on the number of guests expected in the ceremony and what is required to entertain them. The suitor pays the cost of the entertainment of the guests to the bride's family while he buys all the kola nuts and drinks required for the occasion.

On the appointed day the family of the suitor carries the kola nuts, assorted drinks and a dance troupe to the bride's home. On arrival, the usual pleasantries are exchanged by the hosts and guests. Prayers are said by the father of the bride or his representative. The bridal train made up of the bride's age-grade members, in a dance formation, goes out to receive the guests. After this welcome ceremony by the bride's age grade members, entertainment starts amid dancing, eating and drinking.

As the entertainment of guests is going on, the father of the bride or his representative presents a cup of palm wine to the bride and asks her to give it to her proposed husband usually sitting among the guests. The bride in the company of the bridal train looks for her proposed spouse. When she finds him, she kneels down by his side, sips the wine and gives it to the proposed spouse. The spouse receives the wine and drinks it. The crowd cheers in approval and both spouse and bride followed by the bridal train go to the dance floor to celebrate their successful completion of the traditional marriage act. Money-presents are sprayed on the just-married couple by the guests.

From the dance floor the bride goes to sit with the spouse and his people, and from here she goes home with the spouse. Before she leaves the venue of the ceremony, the father of the bride or his representative takes a cup of palm wine, with the bride kneeling or squatting by his side and says prayers of thanksgiving to God and wishes the bride farewell and goodbye. He puts the empty palm wine pot on her head and wishes her safe journey. From here the bride says goodbye to her family and leaves the venue in the company of her new husband with her age grade members singing farewell songs for her.

Chapter Ten

CHILD ADOPTION IN THE IGBO FAMILY SYSTEM

The adoption of a child in Igboland is the traditional acceptance of a child as a member of the family of the adopting man or woman. Adoption in Igboland is as old as the Igbo community which existed many centuries before European influence on the West Coast of Africa. During those early years of existence of the Igbo community, adoption was by a member or friend of a child's extended family and the adopted child continued to bear the family name of his/her biological parents. Marriages were contracted between spouses who were mostly natives of one ancestral village or town and everybody was regarded as members of one large extended family. A married woman who was called by her husband's first name as wife of Mr. 'A' or wife of Mr. 'B' continued to bear her biological father's name in her married life.

The preservation of family names was an important issue in Igbo culture. Our ancestors believed that the main reasons for marriage were two fold; to beget male children who would extend their families and bear their family names, and female children who would get sons to bear their husband's family names. Marriages that did not produce male children were regarded as failures.

Traditional marriage in Igbo culture was like an exulted adoption of a woman by another family. The importance attached to this relationship can be seen in the time taken to negotiate it, the number of people involved in the negotiation, the marriage norms observed, the amount of bride-wealth paid, and the traditional rites observed. In this culture, every family strove to have as many members as possible in the family who would constitute a strong fighting force, and many family hands for the procurement of their daily bread. The more blood related the members of the extended family were, the more secure and reliable their family tended to be and the more formidable their unity of purpose was.

Every capable member of the family made it a point of duty to lend a hand of fellowship to the less privileged members of his or her extended family. Well-to-do male members of the family were encouraged to take more than one wife who would be expected to bear many children especially males. Widowed wives were also encouraged to remarry as second, third or even forth wives to other male relatives of the dead husbands so that their productive capacities would remain in their husbands' families. Wealthier members of the extended families were looked upon to adopt or assist orphaned children or those of poor parents. Adopted children on their part were expected to be good members of the community and were bound to love and respect the adopting families.

Adoption of children in those days took one of the following forms under the watchful eyes of the community elders.

a)   An orphaned child was adopted by any willing member or friend of the child's extended family.

b)   In the second marriage of the mother of a fatherless child, the new husband usually adopted his wife's child and brought him/her up as his biological child

c)   A tradesman often adopted a child as an apprentice to his trade without any charges and took care of the child till the end of his apprenticeship and until his maturity as an adult.

d)   During the Nri civilization which lasted for nine centuries (AD 800-AD 1700) religious families often dedicated their children to a deity for worship or protection purposes. The children were brought up within the cult community which was usually near the shrine of the deity but they kept their biological fathers' names.

After the arrival of European influence, to Igboland in the 16th century through trade and evangelization, several changes took place in the Igbo traditional community life especially in Igbo marriages and the adoption of children. After the introduction of the Atlantic slave trade into Igboland by European traders, many families were hard hit by poverty and bereavement as a result of inter-settlement wars and slave raids. Many children were abandoned by dead, kidnapped or fleeing parents.

Many relatives of the dead or kidnapped parents who could not find legal adoptions for these abandoned children were forced by the situation to leave the children to die of poverty or sold them to slave agents who brought them up in slave camps as domestic slaves or sold them later into slavery. By the 19th century when the slave trade was internationally abolished, evangelization came into Igboland and spread the gospel of forgiveness, love and brotherhood, to soften the anger of gravely maltreated individuals, and families who lost loved ones.

Polygamy which was the order of the day before European influence started to give way to the era of one man one wife which consequently reduced adoptable child- population in Igboland. This new era of one-man one-wife gave women more confidence in, and more commitment to marriage, and they proudly started to bear their husband's family names. Rejected or abandoned babies who were earlier thrown into rivers or lakes; or left in the bush to die during the slave trade are now accepted and taken care of by religious organizations or by humanitarian bodies. These rescued babies are now legally given out for adoption where they are loved and they bear the family names of their adopting families.7

Chapter Eleven

EVALUATION OF THE EXTENDED FAMILY SYSTEM AS ESTABLISHED BY OUR ANCESTORS

In this discussion we shall try to show that the vision of our ancestors in establishing their own concept of a social security system was achieved in the running of the traditional marriage in Igbo family system. We should remember that it took a lot of trial and error efforts to establish this family system. This evaluation shall take us to the fact that the system was established by our earliest ancestors for the survival of their small population many centuries before European influence.

These earliest ancestors gave this system the strength of an unwritten constitution or way of life which every family was traditionally duty-bound to carry with it to its various extending families or settlements. The community elders were then given the traditional mandate to oversee the working of Igbo marriages and to ensure the effectiveness of the institution in the running of the Igbo family system.

As various Igbo families moved apart and established their own settlements, the marriage norms as established by the earliest ancestors were reviewed and little amendments were allowed to accommodate immigrant views and to upgrade the Igbo marriage norms in order to represent current social developments. When the Europeans came to the African West Coast for trade, they also introduced new ideas to the marriage institution, such as, court and church marriage rites, and the payment of bride-wealth with European money. Igbo elders reviewed the Igbo marriage rites again to accommodate European ideas and rites in the final stages of the Igbo traditional marriage without changing the basic substances of Igbo marriage norms.

At the moment the Igbo traditional marriage institution is still active, in the successful contracting of Igbo marriages, and the enhancement and protection of the extended family system. The fact that a lot of Igbo youths travel to various cities of the world today in search of education, employment or trade has not removed the importance attached to various aspects of the Igbo traditional marriage. Although this situation has created room for modernization and abridgment, or combination of stages of marriage ceremonies, it has not adversely affected the usual intensity of the Igbo social system and the extended family relationships. The Igbo family and town unions are still alive and strong at home and in many cities of the world, breaking the kola nuts and remembering the words of the elders about Igbo homeland. The celebration of its annual festivals and marriage ceremonies are usually among the top items of discussion.

Most of the original rites and ceremonies instituted into the Igbo traditional marriage by our ancestors, such as the use of kola nuts, palm wine and money during the contracting of Igbo marriages are still in use today. The involvement of many members of the extended families of both sides to the proposed marriage negotiation is still in place. The mutual exchange of gifts and visits between the proposed bride and bridegroom before marriage as established by the ancestors is still maintained today as the most beautiful aspects of the Igbo marriage system irrespective of the fact that these marriage norms have weathered centuries of reviews and amendments by subsequent elders. From the foregoing, one can see that the most beautiful aspects of the Igbo traditional marriage system envisaged by the ancestors to give social security to the extended family system has been maintained for centuries.

Chapter Twelve

EROSION OF THE EXTENDED FAMILY SYSTEM

The past generations of the Igbo nation had endeavored to protect the extended family system because it was established by their ancestors as the Igbo social security system. They had also ensured that their other cultural institutions, established by the ancestors were protected from the abrasive activities of foreign cultures and values.

In this effort, the Igbo had, as a matter of priority protected the Igbo traditional marriage institution which gave birth to the male and female kinship matrices that produced the extended family system. These two kinship matrices produced the social system which had no fixed number of nuclear family units but produced clusters of blood relatives. These clusters of relatives may have been geographically separated by marriage but were closely tied to their extended family units. The children of these two kinship matrices shared great mutual respect, assistance, protection, and obligations in their ancestral kinship connections and the extended family units.

When Europeans came to the West Coast of Africa

towards the middle of the 15th century, they introduced export and import trade to the Igbo who had been involved in internal trade by barter prior to European and Arab contacts. The use of money which the Europeans introduced fascinated the Igbo traders who fell headlong into trade relations with the Europeans. In addition to import and export trade with the natives, the Europeans introduced formal education of Igbo children in primary school subjects, and evangelization on Christian religious beliefs. These new European institutions produced new openings for employment as primary and bible-school teachers, sales assistants to European traders, office workers and drivers in colonial administrative offices.

These new openings attracted Igbo youths who left Igboland in their hundreds every year to other parts of Nigeria, away from members of their extended families and the traditional attractions and protection accruable from the extended family system. The new Christian churches founded by the Europeans, established new religious societies that saw their members as parts-and-parcel of the Christian family. They gave the members badly needed socio-political protection. Living far away from home and away from their traditional extended families, some Igbo youths accepted their new Christian families as alternatives to their traditional extended family units while some others took shelter in workers' unions. These new church-family relationships opened new escape- routes for those youths wishing to cut off the demand, for financial assistance from members of the extended families and town unions at home in Igboland.

Today a substantial portion of the annual income of the Igbo nation comes from outside Igboland, through Igbo business gurus scattered all over the world. As a result, the extended family system has come under a great eroding pressure due to its neglect by these Igbo elders living outside Igboland. In cities all over Nigeria in particular, and all over the world in general there are thousands of Igbo youths involved in all sorts of businesses and controlling sizable amounts of capital. In secondary schools and universities all over the world, the Igbo are there as students and teachers.

The economic successes of the Igbo and the influence of foreign cultures that they are exposed to in the countries of their residence, are affecting their capacity to maintain the extended family networks as established by their ancestors. The Igbo business gurus have palatial buildings scattered all over Igbo towns and villages, that are only used as holiday resorts once or twice every year during the Igbo mass-returns or festivals. Times are changing fast.

> *"All societies, no matter the level of their technological, industrial or sociocultural achievement, have the same genealogical capacity to construct and maintain an extended family. Many do, a few don't, and*

> *some of those who developed an extended*
> *family network, have reversed it because of*
> *the hostility of their changing*
> *environment"⁶.*

"Traveling is part of education" we are told by the elders, and education is a necessary requirement for everybody, to get the leverage one needs to survive in this modern world, but the extended family system must not be sacrificed to achieve these ends. The youth are called upon by the elders to carry the Igbo family culture with them to wherever they live. In view of the foregoing, Igbo youths should not reverse the extended family network in a haste in exchange for European cultures and values. Since the Igbo see themselves as members of one large extended family, their elders did not fold their arms and close their eyes while the cultural achievements of their ancestors are destroyed by the hostility of European civilization.

To achieve above objectives, the "Ohaneze Ndigbo," an apex cultural union of the Igbo nation was formed by the Igbo elders who advised the youth to start close cultural relations wherever they live to maintain the Igbo traditional family networks. This advice resulted in the formation of Igbo town unions wherever a handful of the Igbo resided. These town unions commit their efforts to reviving the Igbo cultural interactions and the renewal of family ties lost

---

6 V. C. Uchendu, 149; Ahiajoku Lecture, Page 40

through occupational integration outside the Igbo culture area.

The age-old mutual protection tendency of members of the Igbo ethnic group can be seen in the observations of Isichei 1976 and Herskovit 1931-20-21, on Igbo slaves in Haiti during the slave trade.

> *Excellent for work in the fields, yet difficult to handle; they kept a strong sense of their Igbo identity and gave help, care and instructions to new arrivals from Igboland.*[7]

The Igbo sense of mutual protection also saved the lives of thousands of Igbo refugees during the Nigerian civil war (1966-1970), when thousands of Igbo people were massacred by fellow country men especially in Northern Nigeria. The Igbo living in the affected towns saw every other Igbo person as brother or sister (Nwannem) and went an extra mile to give assistance and protection when needed. A lot of successful Igbo people today owe their survival and success in life to the generosity and protection of the extended family system.

On top of all the effort being made to preserve Igbo culture and traditional values, westernization and modernization are slowly and silently reducing the

---

7   Elizabeth Isichei 1976 and Herskovit 1931 20-21

intensity of the influence of the extended family system on the Igbo cultural values. Some children who are born and bred outside Igboland grow up as adults without ever visiting Igboland let alone knowing the names of their villages and towns. They can not speak the Igbo language and do not know other members of their immediate family units other than father, mother and siblings. They find it difficult to interact culturally with home people if they go home. Such children could be counted as lost to Igbo culture because neither their language nor their cultural behavior can identify them as Igbo children outside Igboland.

Having this situation in mind, the Igbo have great need to revive this dying institution in their own cultural interest. Whatever school the children attend and wherever they live, Igbo children should be taught to speak the Igbo language at home and recognize members of the extended family by sight and by name as soon as they can do so. Occasions for interaction with other members of the extended family, as in greetings and visits should be encouraged by parents and elders especially during festivals and vacations. The ancestors who established the extended family system many centuries ago expected that Igbo parents should make it a point of obligation to teach their children by their own life style.

The cultural values of the extended family system

such as the exchange of gifts and visits during festivals should be emphasized in all sociocultural activities by Igbo parents and elders as two important strands of Igbo culture. It is the duty of Igbo elders to refurbish these strands of their culture, project and market them for consideration and recognition first by their own people, their neighbors and then the modern world.

In all public life, Igbo parents, leaders and employers of labor should not misplace the promotion of the extended family system, by the award of honor or the employment of labor to any unqualified person, merely because the person involved is a member or friend of the extended family. This behavior, if not checked, betrays Igbo belief and orientation in meritorious achievements in all spheres of human effort, which the Igbo exhibits in all areas of competition, be it western education, political leadership or sports. The extended family system which the ancestors instituted for the protection of Igbo culture and values should rather continue to protect and highlight the Igbo achievement and performance orientation in all areas of human endeavor as an important aspect of Igbo life, and the secret of Igbo successes as a people.

If the extended family system must not be eroded by foreign cultures and values, its members should live up to the vision of the ancestors who instituted the system many centuries ago.

References

Eneze Ruben K.,
Igbo culture.
Published by Author House
1663 Liberty Drive, Bloomington,
Indiana 47403, USA.02/19/2016

Ohadike D. C. Anioma,
A Social history of the Western Igbo
people. Ohio University Press, Athens,
USA 1994.

Onuigbo – Sylvernus,
The history of Ntuegbe Nese Afro-orbis
Publication Ltd. Nsukka, Nigeria.

Onwuejeogwu M A.
Evolutionary trends in the history
of the development of the Igbo
civilization in the culture theater of
Igboland in Southern Nigeria.
1997 Ahiajoku Lecture.

Uchendu V. C. Ezi na Ulo
The extended family in Igbo
civilization. Govt. Printer Owerri,
Nigeria.1995 Ahiajoku Lecture.

CPSIA information can be obtained at
www.ICGtesting.com
Printed in the USA
FFOW01n2247100316
22195FF

ISBN: 978-1-7335505-0-5

www.ingramcontent.com/pod-product-compliance
Lightning Source LLC
Chambersburg PA
CBHW070553030426
42337CB00016B/2478

9781733550505